LOS ANGELES

Where Anything is Possible

Larry Brownstein

About the Author

Larry Brownstein is a contributing editor of Focus on Imaging magazine. He is one of the principal photographers in the book *America the Beautiful* and is featured in the book *Best of Nature*.

He is a frequent contributor and columnist for several photography magazines including Photographic and Rangefinder. His work is represented by several international stock photography agencies including Getty Images, PictureQuest, Rainbow, California Stock, ImageState and New York Stock.

For stock photography requests or to order additional copies of this book, please contact Larry Brownstein at 310-815-1402 or via e-mail at larry@larrybrownstein.com.

Published by:
Brownstein Publishing
P.O. Box 2240
Culver City, CA 90231-2240
Tel: 310-815-1402
www.larrybrownstein.com

ISBN 0-9742633-0-3
Printed in China through Palace Press International
Distributed to the trade by National Book Network:
1-800-462-6420

Preface

You don't need a convertible sports car and a nasty redhead at your side to enjoy Los Angeles, the City of Angels. All you need is an open mind and a sense of adventure.

Los Angeles is diverse - ethnically, architecturally and even geographically (with beaches and mountains). Los Angeles is avant-garde - witness the new Frank Gehry-designed Walt Disney Concert Hall, the modern Acropolis known as the The Getty Center and the controversial new Cathedral of Our Lady of the Angels. The decades-old Theme Building at the airport still looks futuristic!

When my sister and twin nephews were visiting from New York I took them to see the Haute Dog Easter Parade in Belmont Shores. I recall the look on their faces as they enjoyed the canine fashion show - a combination of amusement, amazement and pity for us poor lost souls who would even think of such a thing. But these die-hard New Yorkers enjoyed themselves nonetheless.

At the Doo Dah Parade in Pasadena, I was dancing and weaving around the participants while taking pictures. I was no spectator. I was a participant and I was all lit up with joy being part of this wacky event. A friend of mine spotted me and said he had never seen me look like that before. He had no way of knowing that I had temporarily taken on the persona of Gary Winogrand, one of my photographic heros.

Yes, anything can happen in Los Angeles. It is not a city ruled by logic. New York is a much more logical place, right down to the orthogonal grid of its streets. Los Angeles is not even the most aesthetically beautiful city in California. San Francisco, with its glistening bay, curving streets, and undulating hills gets that distinction. Los Angeles is not dense with emotional overtones as are many European cities. Paris, for example, is the city of art and romance. You can't beat Paris if you want to see a lot of blurry paintings with your sweetie.

But Los Angeles is transcendental, it's spiritual, I would say. (And don't even ask how many gurus I have heard speak in this town.) If spirituality is finding one's own unique, true essence then Los Angeles reflects the spiritual search of its residents. There is no better example of this than Simon Rodia's Watts Towers. In his spare time, using the refuse of society, he expressed his unique creative vision, building his whimsical towers in his backyard. There is no logic or classical beauty to these towers. But, in their own transcendent way they make perfect sense.

So it is with Los Angeles - at first sight it is disorienting with no simple-to-grasp geometrical model to aid in navigation. There are no obvious geographic features to attract tourists. But Los Angeles works at a level beyond the mind and beyond the physical.

The United States is home to the restless souls who felt constrained in their countries of origin. And Los Angeles is home to many of those souls who felt too constrained in New York, Duluth, Kalamazoo, Tallahasee and Tuba City - because anything is possible in Los Angeles.

Venice Beach

For a total immersion in the city's multi-ethnic, hyper-realistic, creative exuberance there is no better place than Venice Beach. Here you'll find drum circles, skate-dancers, performance artists, comedians and the run-of-the-mill exhibitionists showing off enough tattoos, pierced body parts and rainbow-colored hair to draw police attention anywhere else.

Venice is tremendously entertaining and a magnet for tourists. But don't be fooled into thinking that Venice is just another synthetic playground. Venice is a real community with Korean shop-keepers, a Jewish synagogue and even authentic canals. And the beach is nice too.

VENICE BEACH

Hippie Man

VENICE BEACH | *After the Storm*

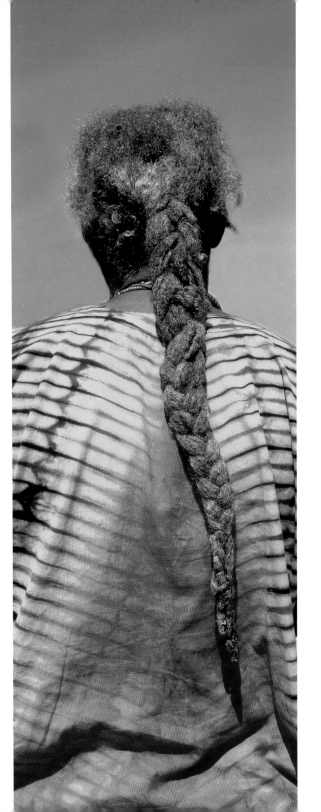

VENICE BEACH
Musician with Dreadlocks

VENICE BEACH | *Venice Pier*

VENICE BEACH | *Pizza Man*

11

VENICE BEACH
Boy Posing with Macaws

VENICE BEACH | *Man in Red*

VENICE BEACH | *Tattooed Woman*

VENICE BEACH
Mural

VENICE BEACH
Festival of the Chariots

Sights & Landmarks

Things are not always as they seem in this town. The LAX Theme Building masquerades as a futuristic spaceport though it is actually a restaurant. The Queen Mary in Long Beach looks seaworthy but hasn't budged for decades. Its former neighbor, the Spruce Goose, was sometimes described as a "flying boat" though it never flew more than a few minutes and certainly never floated. King Kong hangs threateningly over Universal CityWalk but no one seems concerned. So don't waste too much time trying to make sense of things in the city where anything is possible. Just enjoy the view!

LAX INTERNATIONAL AIRPORT

LAX Theme Building

UNIVERSAL CITY
Universal City Walk

SUNSET BLVD.
Billboards and Traffic

LAX | *Light Cylinders*

LAX
Plane Landing

20

UNIVERSAL CITY
Billboard and Murals

DOWNTOWN
Pershing Square

DOWNTOWN | *Office Buildings*

DOWNTOWN
Skyline with 110 Freeway and Overpasses

DOWNTOWN | *Skyline*

SANTA MONICA | *Pier Entrance at Ocean Ave.*

CENTURY CITY
Office Buildings and Traffic

DOWNTOWN | *Skyline with 10 Freeway*

HOLLYWOOD | *Pantages Theatre*

MELROSE AVENUE
Neon Reflections

DOWNTOWN | *View from Baldwin Hills*

HOLLYWOOD BLVD.
With Christmas Lights

LONG BEACH | *The Queen Mary*

HUNTINGTON BOTANICAL GARDENS
Japanese Garden

HUNTINGTON BOTANICAL GARDENS
18th Century Statuary

Parades, Festivals & Celebrations

The Doo Dah Parade, in Pasadena, is the quintessential Los Angeles event - a monumental outburst of creative expression. A Charlie Chaplin impersonator is often seen waddling around. An Uncle Fester look-alike can be seen with a light bulb burning in his mouth. The Hibachi Barbeque Grill Team bazooka-launches baked potatoes into the crowds while roller skating waitresses serve hot dogs with a squirt of mustard. And the Precision Briefcase Drill Team, dressed like so many Alan Greenspans, swing their briefcases like drum majorettes.

From Pow Wows to Gay Pride parades to Carnaval and ethnic celebrations, it is all to be found in L.A., where anything is possible.

THE DOO DAH PARADE

Fishy Man

POW WOW
Man in Ritual Dress

THE DOO DAH PARADE | *Family in Car*

THE DOO DAH PARADE | *The Bride*

THE DOO DAH PARADE
Painted Car

THE DOO DAH PARADE | *Charlie Chaplin Impersonator*

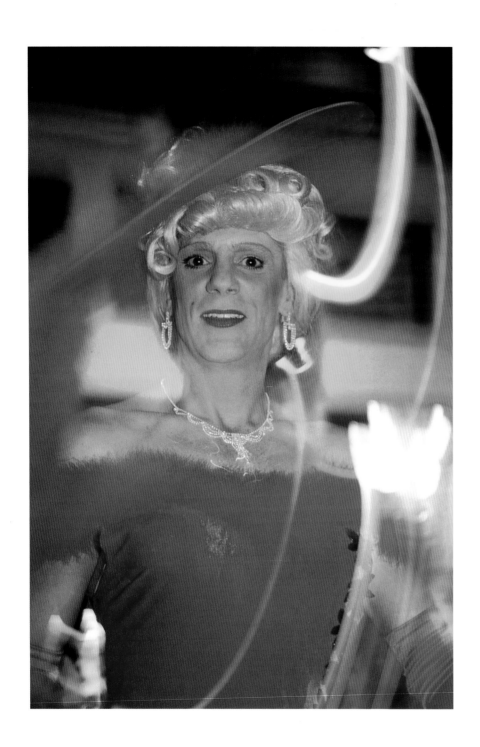

WEST HOLLYWOOD HALLOWEEN CARNAV.
Man in a Red Hat

WEST HOLLYWOOD HALLOWEEN CARNAVAL
Rock Star

RENAISSANCE PLEASURE FAIRE | *The Bordello*

THE ROSE PARADE
Marching Band

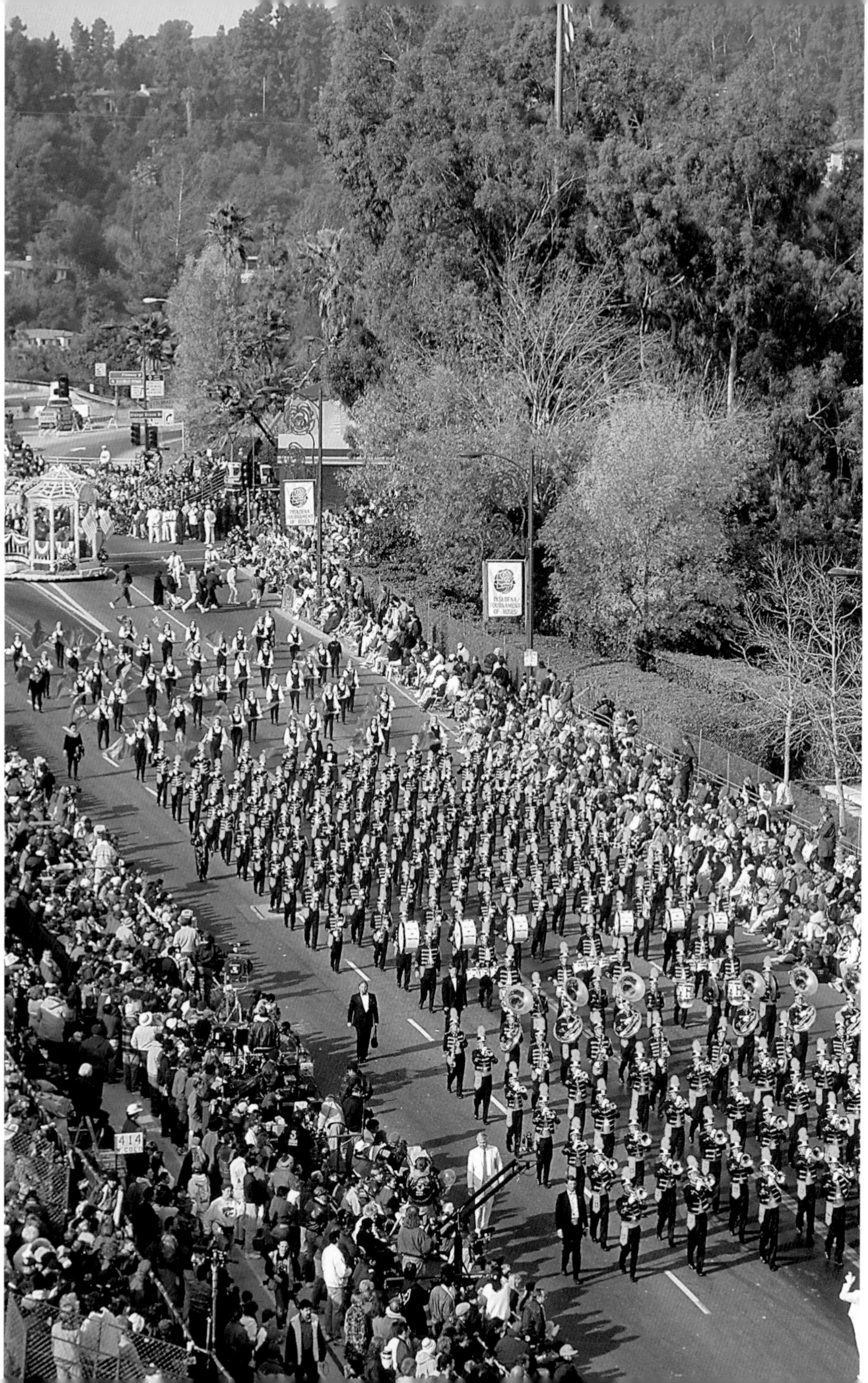

THE ROSE PARADE | *Bouquet*

THE ROSE PARADE | *Flower Girl*

LONG BEACH CARNAVAL
Dancer in Parade

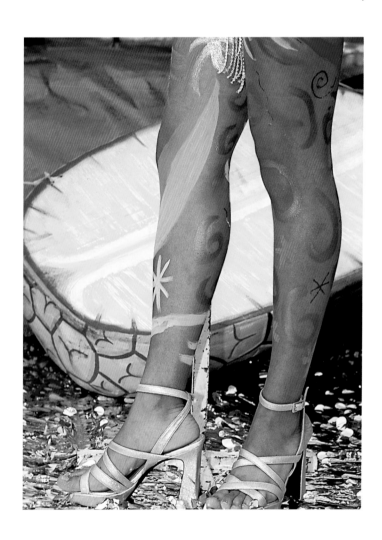

FESTIVAL OF THE CHARIOTS, VENICE BEACH | *Traditional Dance*

HAUTE DOG EASTER PARADE
The Hawaiians

WEST HOLLYWOOD GAY PRIDE PARADE | *Geisha Man*

ABSOLUT CHALK STREET PAINTING FESTIVAL
Woman with Flowers

ABSOLUT CHALK STREET PAINTING FESTIVAL
Old Man

Architecture

With mosques and cathedrals, kitschy theme restaurants and grand monuments, L.A. architecture runs the gamut of styles.

It looks as though God himself dropped the giant donut that is embedded into the roof of Randy's Donuts in Westchester. Or perhaps a giant alien inadvertently let a tasty treat get away.

Simon Rodia, an Italian immigrant, spent his days doing manual labor and all his spare time collecting society's debris - broken bottles, tiles, plates, etc. - and assembling it all into his solo architectural masterpiece in Watts. Is it possible that one untrained, uneducated man could build such an inspiring monument by himself in his spare time? Yes, it is!

WATTS TOWERS
by Simon Rodia

T DISNEY CONCERT HALL

Construction Site

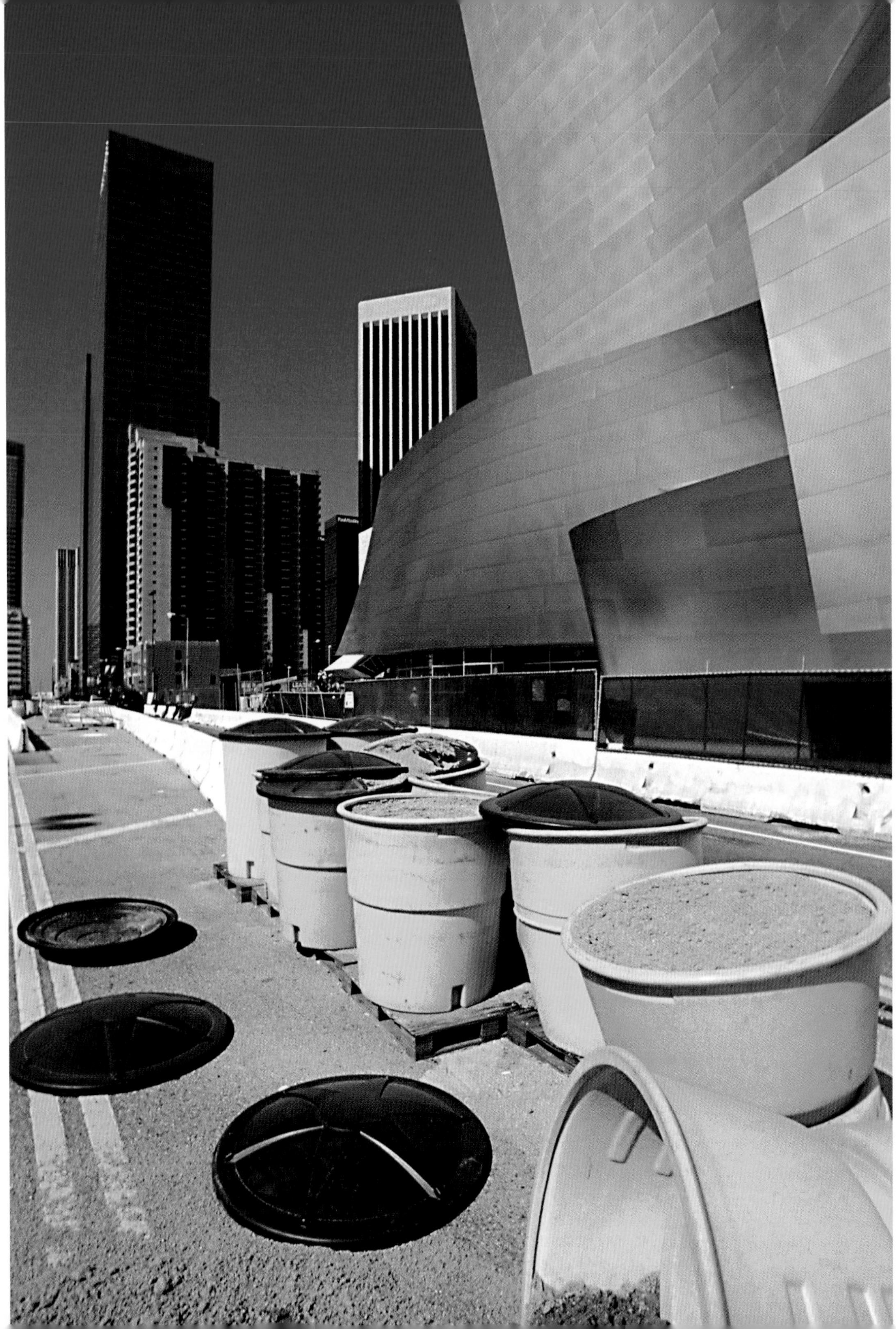

GRIFFITH OBSERVATORY
From Borchart Ridge

GRIFFITH OBSERVATORY
Moonrise over City

ELEVATOR DOOR
Downtown Office Building

EASTERN COLUMBIA BUILDING
Art Deco Clock

CALIFORNIA SCIENCE CENTER
Exposition Park

WESTIN BONAVENTURE HOTEL | *Sunset Reflections*

52

HOLLYWOOD
Capitol Records Building

KING FAHAD MOSQUE
Mural Inside the Dome

ST. SOPHIA
Greek Orthodox Cathedral

LAX THEME BUILDING | *Encounter Restaurant*

Amusement Parks

The adventures that await you at Southern California's amusement parks may make you feel as Alice did when she fell into the hole. Enjoy water slides, man-made circular rivers (how do those currents run in circles?), animatronic animals, comic book heroes and even cities made out of Legos. You can jump, slide, splash, spin and frolic with joy at these amusement park playgrounds. Let your child run free and your Inner Child, too.

I brought my daughter to Raging Waters in San Dimas, CA. The temperature was above 110 degrees and a brush fire could be seen in the close vicinity. But no one seemed to notice. It was just a little side show in the land of the possible.

SIX FLAGS HURRICANE HARBOR

The Forgotten Sea

60

LOS ANGELES COUNTY FAIR | *Carousel Detail*

LOS ANGELES COUNTY FAIR
Slide and Ferris Wheel

LOS ANGELES COUNTY FAIR
Carousel Detail

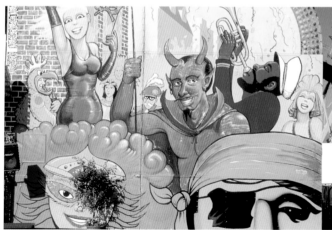

LOS ANGELES COUNTY FAIR
Mural on Amusement Park Ride

SIX FLAGS MAGIC MOUNTAIN | *X Roller Coaster*

The Beach

From the secluded coves in Palos Verdes, to the yacht harbor in Hermosa Beach, to the Baywatch scene of Manhattan Beach (complete with volleyball, surfing and bountiful blondes), to the surfer dudes at Zuma and the colorful crowds on the rides at the Santa Monica Pier, unmatched diversity, fun and games await.

Just when I thought I had seen it all, the last time I visited the Manhattan Beach Pier, I saw a seemingly endless school of dolphins migrating north. Many of them swam within a few feet of the surfers who were sitting on their boards and watching the spectacle.

SANTA MONICA BEACH
Crowds on Labor Day

SANTA MONICA | *Pacific Park and the Pier*

MALIBU
Pier at Sunrise

MALIBU
Pier at Sunset

MALIBU | *Pier at Sunrise*

MANHATTAN BEACH
Girls Looking at Surfers from Pier

MARINA DEL REY | *Girl Running*

PALOS VERDES
Mustard Fields

EL MATADOR STATE BEACH | *Storm Clearing*

72

SANTA MONICA BEACH | *Sea Gulls*

SANTA MONICA BEACH | *Sea Gulls*

Shopping

New England is known for its quaint antique shops. In the Midwest you can find stores with beautiful quilts and handmade dolls. In the Southwest numerous roadside curio shops sell beautiful Indian jewelry, pottery and rugs.

In this eclectic town you can get all this plus Buddha statues, traditional and avant-garde kimonos, Persian carpets, Danish furniture, sexy lingerie and even a scrap-metal, life-size menagerie - giraffes included.

With Korean, Japanese, Vietnamese, Russian, Orthodox Jewish, Ethiopian, Mexican and other neighborhoods in the city, you can sample cuisine from soul food to kim chi and find merchandise from around the world.

MELROSE AVE.

Mannikins

BROADWAY | *Toys*

THE PROMENADE AT HOWARD HUGHES CENTER | *Christmas Tree*

MELROSE AVE. | *Mannikins*

MELROSE AVE. | *Neon and Glass*

MELROSE AVE. | *Neon Signs*

VENICE BEACH | *Buddhas and Beads*

NICK METROPOLIS | *Marilyn and Elvis*

ARON'S RECORDS
Staircase

Sports

With beautiful weather year-round, it is no wonder that there are so many beautiful, tanned bodies here as people enjoy volleyball, swimming, mountain biking, surfing, windsailing, etc.

You can surf Malibu in the morning and hike in the Santa Monica Mountains in the afternoon. Or, perhaps, you'll do some dance skating with the brothers in Venice in the A.M. and drive a couple of hours to Big Bear for skiing in the P.M.

Or will it be a bike ride on The Strand in the South Bay? Or perhaps a swim, tennis ... How to decide when there are so many choices?

HERMOSA BEACH

Volleyball Tournament

BLOCK PARTY
Shootin' Hoops

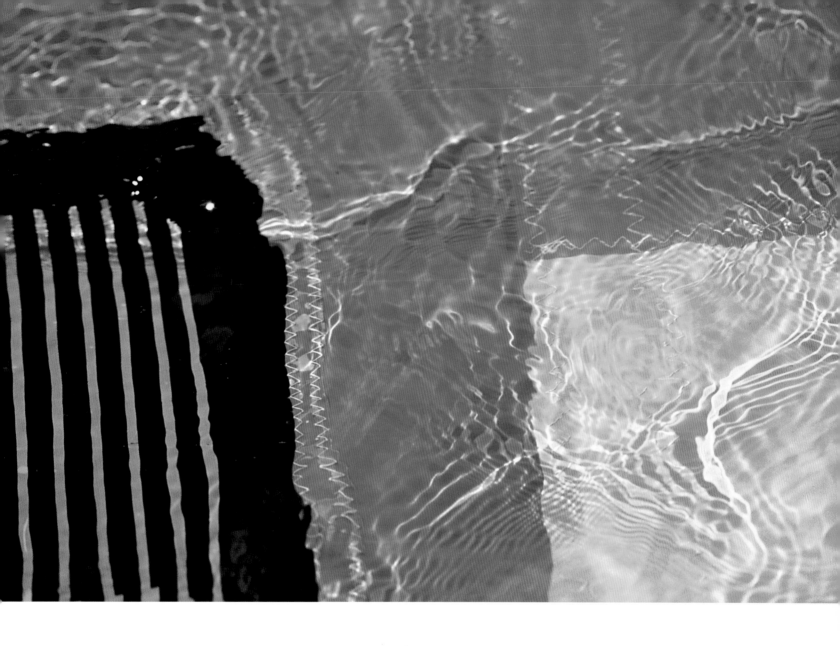

LEO CARRILLO STATE BEACH | *Windsurfing Sail*

ZUMA BEACH
Triathlon

MALIBU CREEK STATE PARK
Mountain Biking

ZUMA BEACH | *Swim Race*

UNIVERSITY OF SOUTHERN CALIFORNIA | *Swim Meet*

LEO CARRILLO STATE BEACH | *Windsurfing*

Cars

Los Angelenos love their cars. Whether it is a Lamborghini Countach, a Ferrari Testarossa, a classic Stingray Corvette, an old Chevy or a car just off the lot, people are very conscious of their cars. You don't find that many old beat up cars here.

In the last few years there has even been a trend towards art cars. I have seen a van with hundreds of old, plastic cameras mounted on it. I saw another van covered with small brass statuettes.

There are more Japanese and German cars than American cars in L.A. I imagine Los Angelenos find American cars so ordinary. And who would want an ordinary car in such an extraordinary city?

CAT CAR
Lotus Festival, Echo Park

ART CAR | *Hollywood*

"WOODIE" | *OceanFest, Oceanside*

ORANGE BEETLE | *Aron's Records*

14/5 FREEWAY INTERCHANGE | *Santa Clarita Valley*

YELLOW VAN | *Venice Beach*

OLD CHEVY, MEN WITH DOGS | *Gay Pride Parade*

Acknowledgments

Superficially, this book is about Los Angeles. However, on another level, this book is about creativity, inspiration and transcendence. I hope that this book can be a reminder that we can do more than just follow the pack. We can listen to our hearts and create our dreams. It is my hope that this book will inspire some to commit to the project that is keeping them up at night.

I want to thank my mother, Ruth Brownstein, who taught me to think for myself and to keep on learning. I thank my father, Joe Brownstein, for his devotion to the family. I thank my wife, Marge, who has always loved and supported me and I thank my daughter, Sophie, for making me a kid again. A special thanks to photographer Harry Peronius who started me on this path. I was 24 when I went to Asia with Harry and I had never owned a camera until we landed in Hong Kong. I bought a Minox camera with a Zeiss lens and was instantly smitten. A lot of film went through that camera in China, the Philippines, Thailand, Burma and India. And I have been passionate about photography ever since.

I would also like to thank Bill and Estelle Balopole, Robert Balopole, Peter Bennett, Alicia Elkort, Martin Elkort, David Fairrington, Kieran Fulkerson, Ron and Mary Hulnick, Bill Hurter, Rick Indenbaum, Mary Kalifon, Marce Kelly, Matt MacConnel, Lin Morel, Carolyn Ryan, Marla Dishman Wein and Jeff Zimerman for their contributions to this book.

-Larry Brownstein, Culver City, CA, September 2003

Credits:

Arthur Secunda, *Angel Light, Angel Bright* statue on page 2.
R. Cronk, *Venice Reconstituted* mural on page 14.
Christopher Ulrich, street painting on page 47.

Cover Photo:

Walt Disney Concert Hall. Used with permission. Thanks to Elizabeth Hinckley/LA Philharmonic.